# HOW TO SURVIVE

# Eating Disorders

**Book #8 in HOW TO SURVIVE SERIES**

## Stephanie Anne Allen

Copyright

April 9, 2019

# Contents

## Preface

Hello my friends! Welcome to the 8th book in the How to Survive Series. I'm glad you have decided to read or listen to this book, as it will guide you on your journey of recovery from your eating disorder. This book will offer you hope, encouragement, inspiration, insight, and tips on how to cope successfully with any eating disorder including anorexia, bulimia, and binge-eating disorder.

This self-help book is proceeded by 7 others in the series on depression, bipolar disorder, schizophrenia, anxiety, BPD, PTSD, and schizoaffective disorder. The How to Survive Series is second to my amazing, thought-provoking, intriguing, intimate, compelling true story titled My Mental Madness Memoir. This book takes the reader deep into the depressed, manic, and psychotic mind. It is totally unique and one-of-a-kind. There is no other book out there quite like that one.

I write my books from a compassionate and empathetic point of view. I've been there. Done that. I am straight-forward and 100% honest. I care about my readers and all my fellow humans.

I share what I know to help others. I want people to know that they are not alone, that I care, and that there is a way through any obstacle. I want others to fight the battle until it is won.

Never give up. You have so very much to live for. You have so many contributions to give to this world. Everyone is on this Earth for a reason. We all should fulfill our purpose and live to the best of our ability.

Life is hard, but it is never impossible. We need to lean on one another. Alone we are strong, but together we are even stronger. Connect with others who suffer, and you will find that strength that you have been longing for. The strength will come when you least expect it.

Many people find strength through faith. God cares. He is there. He wants the best for us. We are worthy of His love and grace. He will never turn His back on you. He holds you securely in His arms.

In addition to faith, the other 4 components of recovery are courage, strength, hope, and love. Courage lies within you. Fear not. And those with true courage have conquered all fear. Fear not that you won't get through this. Fear not that it could kill you.  Fear not because God is with you!

Strength is earned from overcoming past difficulties.  You survived 100% of your problems, and you will overcome this as well.  Your hardships have allowed you to wear a full protective armor, of sorts.

Hope comes when we trust that things will work out.  It might not be instantly.  But there is hope that God will allow for us a better and brighter tomorrow.

Love is the most powerful force ever.  If you have love, you have everything.  But it must be a love without condition.  The source of that love may well be God.  But you can also find that love within yourself.  You can learn to love yourself.  You can then seek out love from others.  Unfortunately, others may never be able to love you the way you want and deserve.  You must use love to allow you to feel worthy of courage, faith, strength, and hope.  Love will open your eyes to so many beautiful things.

You are on the verge of finding the most incredible love within you.  You have taken a major step forward in choosing to read this book.  Read with the intent to allow this book to help you to recover.  Read it for yourself and not because you feel forced to by someone else.  This book is a wonderful tool for you to use.  It offers you tips and guidelines you will be able to use instantly to help you in your recovery.

You are not alone.  I've been there.  Thousands of others have been there as well.  Please never give up.  Life is a beautiful thing, and you will see that more clearly once you have overcome your eating disorder.

There is hope!

# Chapter 1

## What Are Eating Disorders

Eating disorders are mental health disorders that cause both physical and emotional turmoil in the sufferer.  Eating disorders include anorexia nervosa, bulimia nervosa, and binge-eating disorder.

Eating disorders often occur because of the victim may obsess over their weight, body image, and may develop a negative relationship with food. Factors in the prevalence of eating disorders include biology, family history, and the pressures of complying with the social norm (often mistaken by the victim).

These disorders tend to most commonly affect women in their teens and 20s.  But it can affect anyone from young to old and either sex can be inflicted with an eating disorder.

Eating disorders can cause a great deal of harm to someone's physical health, including heart problems and digestive issues.  Also, they can affect a person's bones, and may lead to and cause other diseases as well.

Eating disorders do have a huge effect on the mental wellbeing of the patient. Not only can they be caused by mental illness, but they can affect your existing mental illness by causing it to worsen and become out of control. Co-existing conditions may include depression and anxiety.

Due to the severity of the eating disorder, it is very important to seek professional treatment immediately. You will need a primary physician, a psychiatrist, a therapist, and a nutritionist. If the disorder has caused damage to your other body systems, treatment from a specialist may be required.

It is very important to remember that this isn't something you should try to hide. It is not your fault. Through the help of your mental health team you should be able to get yourself back on track. They will enable you to see your issue and to focus on correcting it. They with let you explore your relationship with food and build a more realistic view of your body. They will help you form a better relationship with yourself. And they will even help you realize that you are number one in your life.

Eating disorders can destroy the victim by tearing them apart both physically and psychologically. They can lead to many medical and mental conditions. And you can die from it if you do not seek treatment. You could have a heart attack or even commit suicide as a result of co-occurring depression.

But there is hope! And you are worth it! You can and you will overcome this. I believe in you.

We will explore the symptoms of eating disorders in the next chapter. This is important in building your knowledge and understanding of eating disorders. This information is vital to your recovery.

Chapter 2

## Symptoms of Eating Disorders

We will focus on three eating disorders each having distinct symptoms. Anorexia nervosa, bulimia nervosa, and binge-eating disorder are the three I will address here.

**Anorexia Nervosa**

Anorexia, for short, is basically an eating disorder in which a person starves their body of its needed nutrients. People with this disorder avoid food at all costs. They also may tend to cling to foods that are extremely low in calories. The typical anorexic has an extremely low body weight, and yet they still believe they are "fat". And they may weigh themselves repeatedly on a scale.

There are two types of anorexia and they include *restrictive* and *binge-purge*. Those with restrictive type put strict regulations on the amount of and type of food they choose to eat. The binge-purge type is the same, plus it adds another factor.  These individuals resort to vomiting, laxatives, and/or diuretics.

Symptoms of anorexia include:

- Extremely underweight
- Unusual eating routines/restrictive
- Abnormal fear of gaining weight
- Excessive exercise
- Obsession with losing weight
- Distorted body image
- Denying a problem exists
- Purging through vomiting and/or using diuretics and laxatives

If the illness persists and shows no or little improvement anorexia can ultimately lead to death as the body starts to shut down.  This can happen if it is not given the proper "fuel" in which to function correctly.  You cannot drive a car without gas.  And thus, you cannot live without an appropriate relationship with food.  Food is the fuel we all need to function.

**Bulimia Nervosa**

Bulimia is a psychological disorder that can lead to death by causing physical destruction of the body.  Behaviors of an individual with bulimia include eating large amount of food and feeling no control over that situation.  Then they engage in purging of the food often through vomiting, laxatives, or diuretics.  They often are preoccupied with weight and body image. They tend to severely judge themselves. Those with bulimia are often a normal weight or may be slightly overweight.

Symptoms of bulimia include:

- Recurrent episodes of consuming too much food.
- Purging, laxative use, diuretic use
- Feeling no control over when to stop eating and purging
- Chronic sore throat from vomiting
- Swollen glands in neck
- Erosion of teeth
- Digestive problems including acid reflux and intestinal distress
- Dehydration
- Kidney issues due to diuretics
- Electrolyte imbalance which can lead to stroke or heart attack.

**Binge-Eating Disorder**

This eating disorder is characterized by recurrent episodes of overeating, but without purging or laxative and diuretic use. Individuals with this disorder tend to overweight and may even be morbidly obese. (But there are people of normal weight who have this diagnosis.) They may overfill themselves with food. And they eat when they aren't even hungry. They may also eat too quickly and consume too much food as a result. Binging tends to occur at least once a week.

Binging takes a huge effect on the psychological mindset of the victim. Victims often feel embarrassed, guilty, and ashamed of their disorder. They do not exercise excessively or purge in any way to try to ward off the excessive consumption of food.

Symptoms of Binge-Eating Disorder include:

- Eating too quickly
- Overfilling oneself with food
- Eating too much
- Eating when not hungry
- Isolated eating

- Feeling ashamed of eating behavior
- Dieting, regardless of results

Now that we have explored the symptoms of eating disorders, we will move on to investigate the causes of these mental illnesses.  Once again, it's important to know all the facts, as this will help you in your ultimate recovery.

# Chapter 3

## Causes of Eating Disorders

So, you have an eating disorder. You may have questions like: *What caused this? Why did this happen to me? Am I to blame? Am I emotionally weak? Why can't I just stop this from happening?*

People who live in societies that have a great excess of food availability tend to be affected more with eating disorders. Also, causes of these disorders have biological, psychological, and cultural origins.

### Biological Causes

Genes may be a factor in getting an eating disorder. So, it does run in families. Also, chemicals and hormones within the brain may be ajar. There may be a possible malfunction in appetite control, due to the miss firing of chemicals within the brain.

### Psychological Causes

Mental illness can be a factor resulting in an eating disorder. They may have low self-esteem and may have an unhealthy drive to be "perfect". Also, impulsive behaviors may be present. In addition, troubled relationships can be a root of the problem. Also, stress and loneliness can be contributing factors.

## Cultural Causes

Today, we often have a very corrupt view of human beauty. Women are taught that they must measure up or they will be undesirable. We often hear that we are too "fat" to be loved. We are criticized often, and repeatedly do so to our own children.

These are the known possible causes of eating disorders. Now we shall move on and I will tell you my own personal story of dealing with having an eating disorder. I do this to offer others hope and inspiration. I recovered and therefore, I know that you can, and you will, recover too. The important thing is to get your mind right. That is what we are working on.

# Chapter 4

## My Own Personal Struggle with an Eating Disorder

We are all born to be beautiful. I mean how incredible is the human body. Truly it is so very complex, yet beautiful. Everyone has beauty. When God created you, He created a miraculously beautiful creature. God made you, and yes, He made you to be beautiful.

Growing up, we often heard insults from others, saying we are too fat. And we would get repeatedly insulted and teased time and time again by our peers. Sometimes, it would destroy our self-esteem, even when we acted like we didn't care, or it didn't matter.

As adults, we often get judged by our own respective mates or even those we are dating. In this society, we are plagued by hate and judgement. And this eventually can break a person down.

Imagine not feeling good enough to be loved. Imagine believing that the only way someone will love you is if you fit the measurements of a barbie doll.  And if you truly believe that, wouldn't you fight hard to be just like that of a barbie doll?

I never wanted to be like a barbie doll.  But I did have an eating disorder.  I suffered with binge-eating disorder.  I would eat until I was extremely full and miserable physically.  The food was my only go to.  I lost all interest in life, except for food.  I would use food as my crutch.  I would eat, eat, eat, until the mental and emotional pain ended.  But it only was a temporary fix.

And turns out the food never cured anything.  The emotional pain never truly left.  It was just put out of my mind for the brief time that I was consuming large amounts of unhealthy food.  Food was not the answer.

I gained weight quickly during my freshman year in college.  Eventually, over the years, my weight increased rapidly to 500lbs.  I had no choice but to get bariatric surgery.  I would have died.

Eventually you learn that you must eat to live, not live to eat.  And your body must be fueled with healthy food.  A car runs better on premium gas.  And the same with the body.

Exercise is important to keep the body strong. It strengthens all the muscles, bones, and internal organs.

Food won't end your pain. I promise you that. I've battled my demons. I've seen hell. I don't want you to suffer as I did.

Even today I have continued reminders of my battle. I have stretch marks all over. That's what happens when you weigh 500lbs. It's a horrible life to live and I wish it upon no one.

Also, I would like to remark that I have a brother who had anorexia. He weighed 74 pounds at six feet tall. His intestines nearly shutdown. He wouldn't eat and was into heavy use of laxatives. He also suffered from severe depression and suicidal ideations at the same time. So, I understand what it is like to have someone in my life with an eating disorder other than myself.

It's horrible watching someone die from it. And I have been on both sides of the fence. I had an eating disorder and I know someone who does.

This is my story and it's true. Just in case you didn't know, I believe in 100% honesty. The "truth" should always come straight from the heart.

I am now going to present the guidelines that I personally used in my recovery from an eating disorder. These can be applied to any eating disorder, not just the one I suffered from. Hope you take the next chapter to heart as it is certain to assist you in your recovery.

# Chapter 5

## How to Conquer Your Eating Disorder

In this chapter I will examine the techniques I have used, and the tips I have given others, in the process of recovery. These guidelines are sure to help you overcome your eating disorder.

**Admit that you have a problem.** How can you fix a problem if you continue to be in denial as to whether it really exists or not? Please open your mind to at least the possibility that you may truly have an eating disorder. If someone has given you this book, it means they are concerned about you and they care. So maybe you do have an eating disorder. It's at least probable.

**Change your relationship with food.** Whether you eat too much or too little, it's time to rethink the whole concept of food. We need it to survive, so don't starve yourself. And don't eat too much either because that hurts the body as well. Find a happy median. And make healthy choices. If necessary, please seek out the assistance of a dietician. They can help you construct balanced meal plans. Again, eat to live not live to eat.

**Stop purging, using laxative and taking diuretics.** For those with bulimia, this is a must. Vomiting causes acid build up in mouth and throat which leads to sore throat and tooth decay. Laxatives destroy the intestinal lining. And diuretics affect the kidneys adversely. These are unhealthy and certainly not a productive way to deal with anything.

**Use positive self-affirmations.** Tell yourself how great of a person you are. Build yourself up. Tell yourself: "I'm awesome." "I did a good job." "I'm worthy of life." "I have a purpose." "I am loved." This is will help improve low self-esteem that many with eating disorders have. And truth be told you are worthy and have purpose. God put you on this Earth for a reason.

**Keep the faith.** We must always remember to keep faith in ourselves and in God. God has a reason for everything. He allowed you to have an eating disorder, because he has an ultimate plan for your life. You might not understand it now, but someday God will make all our questions answered. You are never alone, because He is with us always. If you don't believe in God, then certainly keep the faith in yourself and your inner being. You can get through this. You overcame all your problems of the past, and you will surely defeat your eating disorder.

**Stay strong and remain hopeful.** Always be ready for anything. Your past battles have strengthened you. Don't forget the lessons you learned through these battles. It is through those lessons that strength increases. And please be hopeful that tomorrow is always a new day filled with new and exciting opportunities. With faith comes hope.

**Have a positive attitude always.** Optimism is the key to living a life worth living. We must find the good in all things, even the things that seem evil and not worthy of any positivity. Things happen, good and bad, but everything has a deeper meaning. And with a positive attitude in life you can get a lot further than with a negative one. You may also obtain more friends that way!

**Take charge of your own life.** It's your life, and you are the master in creating what you want out of it. Don't let others destroy the inner being within you. You know what you want, so go out and grab it. Fulfill your wildest fantasies. Do what you have always wanted to do. Don't let anyone or anything get in your way. You can accomplish anything! And please do not place blame and be resentful of others because of your eating disorder. And do not place blame on yourself either. It is what it is. So, take control and overcome this disorder!

**Limit stressful input.** Stress is a killer. It affects our bodies both physically and mentally. Try to take time out and relax. Never overload yourself. It can lead to a mental breakdown or a heart attack. By limiting stress right now, you will have more time and energy to help yourself in your recovery.

**Obtain a new "beautiful".** I will forever believe that true beauty is on the inside of a person. We can all have pretty eyes, sexy bodies, and be extremely attractive, but that is not true "beauty". Beauty is in the heart. Outer beauty wastes away. But inner beauty can last forever if you nurture it. I see beauty in the way a person thinks, feels, and loves. That is "beauty" to me!

**Seek therapy.** A therapist will assist you in getting your thoughts right. They will guide you in creating better coping skills and problem-solving skills. A therapist will help you with your deep-seated struggle with food and body image, and all other misunderstood emotions and feelings that you may be having.

**Stick to your treatment plan.** Whether your plan was formed by yourself or with the help of a professional, it's important to keep on track and accomplish little goals each and every day. If you have a bad day, don't give up. You will have a good day again. Be strong and give yourself credit. Overcoming an eating disorder is a very hard battle, but you were born to fight it. So, my friend, battle on even when you falter. The rainbow is across the way and I want to see you reach it.

If you follow these tips, you can beat your eating disorder. You have the strength and I gave you the tools. I hope you will use them to the best of your ability. Recovery is possible and we will explore that next.

# Chapter 6

## Recovery and Outcome

The way to eliminate the chance of getting an eating disorder is to prevent it all together. Parents are responsible for the wellbeing of their children. They need to have open lines of communication and need to create an environment in which the child feels comfortable to speak his or her mind. Parents should not act like dieting-junkies around their kids. They need to reinforce, by example, healthy eating and exercising practices. And, if needed, parents should reach out and ask for help from a professional.

If prevention is not an option because the eating disorder already exists, then steps towards proper treatment must be enlisted. Professional assistance is a must if you or someone you know suffers from an eating disorder. Loved ones need to gently urge the victims to seek much needed treatment. Sometimes this is very difficult because victims may not even realize a problem exists. They might retaliate and think that you are the problem.

Eating disorders affect the victim, but they also destroy the victim's loved ones. They may feel truly helpless in this situation. They may be clueless as to how they should help. This is when it is extremely important to seek out a therapist. A rehab center for the victim may be in order. It's important to never give up on your loved one. And it is also very important to never give up on yourself if you are the victim.

With intense therapy and proper intervention, recovering from an eating disorder is entirely possible. You can learn proper eating skills. And in turn, your physical health will improve. And you will feel better as a whole person.

Treatment also will enhance your emotional wellbeing. Many victims have co-existing disorders such as depression, anxiety, and drug use. When we treat the entire person, we are more successful. And often, there is a spiritual side that may be treated as well.

With treatment that revolves around the whole person, we find higher success rates. Therapy helps transform a person's relationship with food and with the individual herself. Once we see a decline in the patient's negative habits, we will see a positive outlook regarding the person's physical health.  And spiritual health gives a person a sense of hope and a reason to see their life as valuable.

So, with proper treatment the outlook for someone with an eating disorder is extremely positive.  You can, and you will, recover from your disorder, if you choose to.  Never give up!  Things may be slow, and you may not feel like you have anything left in you to fight, but trust me, you are stronger than you think.  You do have the will power within you to overcome this.  And you will be the victor in this battle!

I do care and I want you to know that.  You are a warrior and no problem has ever taken you down.  You overcame them all.  Just as you will overcome this one.  The strength, my friend, lies within you.  And I hope treatment will allow you to learn a little about self-love.

Battle on my friends!  This is a war you are guaranteed to win!

# Chapter 7

## My Inspirational Quotes on Eating Disorders

*"Eat to live, not live to eat!"*

I am sure that everyone has heard this one. And it's 100% true. Just as a car needs gas to run, a human needs food to survive. The higher grade of gas, the better your car will run. Just as the healthier food you eat, the better your body will function.

And, surely, we cannot live just to eat food. There is so much more to life than food. Food is a source of life, but if you eat too much or you eat the wrong things, you can run into big trouble. Your body is not made to be over fed. Just as you cannot overflow the gas you put into a car.

*"True Beauty does not lie in the outward appearance of a person. True Beauty is in the mind, heart, and soul of a person."*

You can physically be the most attractive person out there, but if you have a rotten attitude and personality, I won't be interested in you. I investigate the actions and good deeds a person has done, to find true beauty.

*"Even in the darkest of nights, the moon still exists."*

Even when you seem to be fed up and you want to give up, you will find the light. The moon may be hidden behind the clouds, but it is still there. Just as hope if always there even in the deepest thrones of Hell. It is very important to stay hopeful at all times. Hope will allow you to travel through the darkness, because you will anticipate what is to come next in this life.

*"You are loved, worthy, and have purpose."*

Every person was put on the Earth for a very specific reason. God intended us each to fulfill a certain purpose in this world. No person is unneeded. Whether you save lives as a doctor, or you are a secretary, you still have value. Without the role of the secretary, the doctor would not be able to do his job effectively, and if he doesn't do his job correctly, there could be a loss of life.

Therefore, the job of the secretary is just as important.

I believe that being worthy is a birthright!


*"God will not allow any problem to affect you, unless He has a reason to turn that problem into a blessing."*

You may have heard this one too. Basically, God is strengthening you by allowing you to battle your demons. Hardships, problems, difficulties, can all be turned into glory. And God will bestow great blessings upon you. He is building you up for the biggest and best battles in your life. And you will be ready when that battle comes. You will be glorified in the name of God. So, trust God and know that everything happens for a reason. God loves you, and He wants you to be victorious in all you do!

## Author's Note

Dear Friends,

I hope you have found this book to be a valuable part of your recovery or of that of a loved one. I hope you will use the guidelines, I presented, to win your victory over your eating disorder.

This book is preceded by 8 others. My Mental Madness Memoir and 7 books in the How to Survive Series. If you have not read them, I want to encourage you to take a look.

You can beat your eating disorder. I have done so, therefore, I know it is possible and doable. Never give up. There is great beauty inside you. Let that be the beauty you show to the world. And use food as a source of life, not as an enemy or as something that should be put on a pedestal.

Wishing you all the best in your journey of recovery!

Much Love to You All,

STEPHANIE ANNE ALLEN